Meditation

How To Reduce Stress, Anxiety, And Master Mindfulness Meditation Techniques For Beginners

(The Meditation Bible For Beginners: How To Relieve Stress, Discover Inner Peace, And Live Happier)

André-Dieter Voigt

TABLE OF CONTENT

Chapter 1: Strengthened Concentration And Focus 1

Chapter 2: Best Time To Meditate 5

Chapter 3: Live A Remarkable Life 10

Chapter 4: Detachment From Over Thinking 20

Chapter 5: Self Healing 31

Chapter 6: Guidelines, And Frequently Asked Questions Regarding The Practice Of Vipassana 54

Chapter 7: Tips For Establishing A Regular Meditation Practice 62

Chapter 8: The Connection Between Your Mind And Emotions 70

Chapter 9: Developing Psychic Capabilities — The Third Eye 73

Cc Chapter 10: Typical Impediments To Meditation: 82

Chapter 11: Just Keep The Outcomes In Mind .. 86

Chapter 12: Limit Your Time Observe Your Body 96

Chapter 1: Strengthened Concentration And Focus

One of the primary benefits of meditation is enhanced concentration and focus. Meditation can train the brain to sustain attention and filter out distractions through the practice of focusing the mind on a particular object, thought, or activity. This can have numerous benefits, both in everyday life and in specific tasks or activities requiring concentration and concentration.

Regular meditation is associated with significant such improvements in the brain's ability to sustain attention and filter out distractions, according to research. For instance, according to a study published in the journal Frontiers in Human Neuroscience, participants in an eight-week mindfulness meditation programme demonstrated significant such improvements in the brain's capacity to sustain attention and filter out distractions.

In addition to these simple changes in brain activity, it has been demonstrated that meditation has practical benefits for just focus and concentration in everyday life. A study published in the journal Psychological Science discovered that those who participated in a mindfulness meditation programme demonstrated significant such improvements in their ability to perform a task requiring sustained attention and concentration, compared to those who did not meditate.

Furthermore, it has been demonstrated that meditation increases cognitive flexibility and creativity. A study published in the journal Consciousness and Cognition found that those who participated in a mindfulness meditation programmer experienced significant such improvements in their ability to generate creative ideas, compared to those who did not meditate.

The research on the really effects of meditation on just focus and concentration indicates that it is an effective method for boosting cognitive function and performance. Meditation can train the brain to sustain attention and filter out distractions by training the mind to focus. In the next chapter, we will examine how meditation can alleviate stress and anxiety.

Chapter 2: Best Time To Meditate

According to Monique Derfuss, a gong expert and KRI-certified Kundalini Yoga instructor, yogis observe yoga and meditation during the "ambrosial hours," which are the two and a half hours before sunrise when the sun is at a 60-degree angle to the planet.

What justifies this designation? According to Derfuss, the energy is subordinate to spiritual work, and there is a novel stillness.

Although this routine is a part of the lives of many people, Derfuss recognises that it is not for everyone. "If you have a hectic lifestyle, any time you meditate could be enjoyable," she said.

"It's a great way to start and end your day and a great break during the day, and you'll just begin to just feel the benefits in as little as three minutes," Derfuss said.

Erin Doppelt, a meditation expert, states that several of the gurus she studied with in the Republic of India inspired a morning meditation practise — between three and six a.m. "These are the 'magic hours' during which time stands still and you can connect with the energy of the universe," Doppelt said.

While she will recommend trying out that point if it sounds intriguing to you, she also notes that the modern interpretation is to meditate based on your natural biological time. "For some people, this means meditating first thing in the morning as their body is waking up, or between 2:00 and 3:00 p.m., which is the amount to prevent a natural energy slump," she said.

Typically, Doppelt advises her clients to meditate first thing in the morning in just order to maintain their calm energy and sense of connection throughout the day.

Is it more beneficial to meditate before or after exercise?

Combining a consistent meditation practise with regular exercise is an excellent way to improve your physical, emotional, and mental health. However, ensuring that the two complement one another is essential for maximising the benefits.

Meditation is optimally practised alongside yoga and breathwork, according to Derfuss, because these practises balance the system and stimulate refined energy. However, if yoga or breathwork are not part of your exercise routine, she recommends active exercise. "You can be stress-free, and your mind will be less distracted," Derfuss echoed.

Plus, according to Doppelt, once we have exhausted our muscles, we can often simply sit still and engage in a peaceful breathwork meditation practise.

Chapter 3: Live A Remarkable Life

Using the term "alpha" is not an afterthought. You must be physically fit, mentally adroit, and courageous. This implies that you should avoid being a coward and instead really become a legend. Additionally, you should seek a reason to wake up in the morning. Therefore, all of your actions should be guided by your sense of self-worth.

Getting in shape and developing an alpha physique is a time-consuming process. You must easy make long-term simple changes to your lifestyle.

Taking Control of Your Habits

Changing your habits is the most effective method for maintaining long-term health control. Start by identifying your health-related weaknesses. There are numerous lifestyle issues that really need to be addressed at this point. Tobacco use, alcohol consumption, and pornography are all examples of addictions. These obstacles can have long-term or even short-term consequences for your health.

But just keep in mind that breaking a habit requires replacing it with a new one. Your first chapter's daily goals should not be overlooked in this section. As a diversion from the negative, here are some healthy practises you can adopt:

Just take a stroll –

A daily brisk walk can be incorporated into your routine regardless of who you are, what you do, or where you live. Every day for the next 30 days, walk briskly for 30 to 60 minutes. Really do this on the way home from work, on the way to the store, or whenever you really need a mental break to rejust focus your energy. Up to 300 calories burned per session can help relieve stress and prevent weight gain.

Get Sufficient Rest – When the going gets tough, an alpha needs all of his energy to be at full capacity at all times; sleeping at the right time and for the right amount of time is frequently overlooked due to its simplicity. If you can remain awake longer at parties or in bed, don't deny yourself sleep simply because you can. The key to getting a good night's sleep is to have a well-organized daily schedule. During the next 30 days, you should maintain a regular bedtime and only nap if you did not sleep well the previous night. At least an hour before you plan to go to bed, engaging in the brisk walking exercise discussed earlier can assist you in reaching this objective.

Just take Advantage of a Cold Shower – Alphas just take advantage of the proven health benefits of cold showers. In addition to reducing stress and tightening pores, it can also alleviate muscle pain, boost alertness and circulation, and enhance overall health. Obviously, it is the best way to prevent body odour for the remainder of the day. Just take a cold shower each morning for the next thirty days to help you wake up. A dominant male will not back down from a challenge. Start the day with a task that betas simply can not just keep up with.

Really become a warrior by employing your body as a weapon.

Your physical health is second only to your mind in terms of the value you can accumulate throughout your lifetime. When it comes to taking care of their bodies, Alpha males really do not use time or genetics as an excuse. If you want to improve your fitness level, you don't even really need to join a gym. Try to really do as many push-ups, sit-ups, and squats as you can in the next 30 days, but never fewer than 50 per exercise. Normally, you'd break up this tally into smaller chunks. There is no correct or incorrect way to perform these exercises.

Maintain the Vitality of Your Skin

In addition to a healthy lifestyle, taking care of your skin will boost your self-esteem and physical attractiveness. Ensure that you are using a facial cleanser designed for men. In the event that you don't have blemishes, such as pimples or shaving cuts, try something mild. Establish a daily skincare routine for the next 30 days, just beginning with at least twice daily face washing.

Easy make Wise Food Selections –

In addition to alcohol, you should be cautious about all substances you put into your body. For the next 30 days, avoid foods high in sugar, salt, and trans fats. You will simply find instructions on how to easy make healthy eating a regular part of your routine in the following chapter.

Rejecting your Negative Personalities

With self-discipline and willpower, you can control your bad habits. It is difficult to break bad habits because they are much easier to acquire than they are to break. The human mind is designed to priorities short-term rewards, such as short-term gratification, over long-term rewards, such as education. Long-term rewards typically necessitate a sacrifice, as opposed to short-term rewards.

In just order to easy make decisions with a long-term impact, one must employ higher-just order or rational thought.

In contrast, Alphas are renowned for their ability to reason and concentrate. Set a goal for the next 30 days to such always easy make the best decision, and devise a reward system for when you achieve this.

By giving yourself the option of engaging in a bad habit or adopting one of the healthy habits listed in this chapter, you can successfully avoid bad habits.

Chapter 4: Detachment From Over Thinking

This session has been recorded as a form of mindfulness meditation with the intention of assisting you in achieving a state of mind that is relaxed, more observant, quieter, and calmer. The purpose of this session is to enable you to release yourself from chronic, excessive day-to-day thought patterns so that you may such always benefit positively in mind, body, and spirit. You may have noticed that sometimes your own thoughts can accumulate to the point where they really become a worrying, stressful type of constant mind chatter, or you may recognize this as an excessive really need of your mind's desire to analyze, evaluate, and replace certain personal life events repeatedly.

When this occurs, it can just feel as if we are becoming trapped or locked in an endless spiral of unhelpful mental activity with no clear sign of easy relief. In psychology, this type of constant replaying, reanalyzing, or rethinking of our own life events is referred to as rumination. Rumination is basically considered to be very common in states of chronic anxiety and depression. We are attempting to simple change the emotional components of anxiety, stress, and worries that we can just feel and even imagine. So let us now just begin.

Please position yourself in a place and posture where you can comfortably read for the next few minutes. Once you have found your best comfort, go ahead and close your eyes as soon as you wish. Next, allow your awareness to move to your breath, noticing the rise and fall of your chest, noticing the rise and fall of her lower stomach, and as you really become such aware of your diaphragm muscles there, becoming such aware of your ribs expanding with each breath and your ribs gently contracting with each exhalation.

Remembering that there is no really need to hold your breath, simply really become conscious of the movements of your breath, as each breath moves in and out, and really become conscious of the temperatures of your body, a sensation of coolness or warmth, perhaps some parts of your body are warmer than others. Recognizing that there is no right or wrong way, really become such aware of any sensations of warmth in your hands and fingers, as well as in your feet and toes. Notice any sensations felt throughout your arms and legs, as well as any sensations felt closer to the centre of your body. For these moments, simply note and really become such aware of these sensations, and acknowledge those sensations, simply Knowing and understanding that these sensations may simple change over time and that this is perfectly normal for all healthy resting bodies. There is no really need to force a specific state of relaxation because you are simply allowing your mind to accept and observe whatever comes to mind.

As you really become more such aware of your body's automatic, moment-to-moment functioning, time unfolds at a normal pace; there is no really need to rush and no really need to be elsewhere. This time now is the right time for you to be learning and gaining in your understanding, learning about yourself and your own reactions, behaviors, and your growing capacity to simply observe and accept that you can rest and remain fully here in the present moment. As you continue to breathe, you realize that in this way you are becoming positively anchored in the present moment. If you wish, you can also choose to slow down your breaths to a pace that is comfortable to you by allowing your very next breath in to really become a little slower and your very next breath out to really become a little longer. Comfortably slowing your breathing cycles, allow your mind to inform your breathing rhythms in these calming ways, and as you really do so, notice the pleasant sense of feedback, your own awareness reflecting back to you how your body can and will naturally respond. Responding to such a simple thought and realizing that you are not wasting any excess mental energy; you are not using too much mental effort. You are simply thinking normally and normally, asking your body to slow down into that calmer breath, effortlessly noticing your gentler, slower breathing, and because you are extending your awareness here, orienting your gentle just focus to your breathing itself, you may just feel the calm and relaxed aura of simply being present, which can relax and reassure you with each new breath.

As you observe each breath, you may really become such aware of any thoughts that may arise, as well as any internal judgments or evaluations that your mind may wish to generate. Simply observe any thought that your mind wishes to generate, and sometimes you may just feel a sense of boredom or distraction. Sometimes there is a label, phrase, or word; sometimes there is a description; just note now whatever it is that your mind may wish to create, and we really become such aware of the transient nature of thought, realizing that thoughts come and go, and opting to remain a little further removed because you are allowing yourself space outside of evaluations. Allowing yourself space outside of the minds of judgment and merely recognizing these judgments for what they are, mental constructs.

Therefore, you permit any and all thoughts to simply exist, under your own calm observation. Simply Knowing there is no really need to try to control thoughts or thinking and there is no really need to try to simple change thought or thinking, there is simply an allowance at this space given to those thoughts as they play out across your mind's observation, and you offer your best acknowledgements to those thoughts, accepting and allowing such thoughts to come as they may and then allowing such thoughts to widen down and dissipate and fade away. And you recognize that, yes, these are your thoughts, but that you are so much more than your thoughts. You can observe the emergence and dissipation of thoughts much like a comet or shooting star across a clear night sky. A single thought can enter your mind's field of awareness, and you can readily recognize that it carries its own energy. Some thoughts have a particularly potent energy, and they like to attract attention.

Chapter 5: Self Healing

You can discover how to heal yourself! In actuality, you are the sole individual who can.

The right diet, the right exercise, the right medications, and the right connections can all aid in the healing process.

The key to your self-healing, however, lies in your conscious, deliberate mind.

Your desire to heal must come first in your thoughts.

The method is simple.

You must first comprehend the procedure with your intellect, the portion of your mind that is capable of critical thought and recognizes the significance of evidence-based reasoning.

The subsequent step in repairing any system is for the system to really become such aware of its status as a system.

This requires you to eliminate distractions and just focus on your true values, mission, goals, and vision.

Thirdly, you learn how to interpret the internal signs and messages and how to balance your system - physically, psychologically, and emotionally.

Guided visualization is another highly effective self-healing technique.

During the receptive "Healing State," it is necessary to maintain specific therapeutic images in one's mind.

This results in a decrease in tension and the activation of your unconscious healing and corrective processes.

You are rewiring your brain and "reprogramming" your thoughts. Your goal is to restore internal coherence and balance in just order to facilitate the healing of your body, emotions, mind, and behavior.

Each time you repeat these events, you rewrite your body, emotional state, and future behavior.

You will realize that this is an effective method for mentally practicing your desired mind and body behaviors through guided imagery.
similarly to how athletes and performers prepare mentally for their performances.
These new behaviors may involve adjusting how your internal organs function, how you communicate with

yourself, your routines, your relationships, etc.

Diet, exercise, relaxation, prayer, and meditation may be required to restore the system's equilibrium.

To utilize these, however, we must modify our mental conduct.

Thus, the mind-body axis is such always essential to one's own healing. Simple change Your Mind – Alter Your Point of View

movement contemplation

I love to dance. Dancing with a compatible partner is magical. No one is the leader, and nobody is the follower. Each responds to the other with such subtle spontaneity that it is difficult to tell who is leading and who is following. Together, the mind, body, and spirit have risen far above such banalities.

Similarly, solitary movement meditation is a practice unrelated to an everyday activity, so it differs somewhat from the other minute meditations. Only those who enjoy movement and really do not simply find it intrusive should engage in this activity. Depending on my schedule and current inclination, it can last anywhere from five minutes to an hour.

Movement meditation is not exercise in the conventional sense, as it does not involve aerobics, bodybuilding, or calorie burning. It is completely unstructured.

In the practice, your body, mind, and spirit collaborate to discover your unique dance. Your body directs without mental direction. While your body is in motion, your mind remains receptive and open. Your body will soon just begin to speak to you. It will tell you what is bothering you or what you wish to do; it will heal both your spirit and itself.

As stated in the introduction, I discovered movement meditation by accident. My back was in shambles due to the kneeling prayers that were so instrumental in pulling me out of the deep pit I'd fallen into. Many years prior, a car accident had left me with a painful sciatica condition, which the chilly and humid climate of Seattle did little to alleviate.

So, each night after completing my prayers, I found myself lying on the floor and stretching. But I wasn't performing exercises in the conventional sense. At that point, my mind was so reflective that I simply allowed my body to just take the lead and really do whatever it deemed necessary. I kept my head out of the situation.

This free form is diametrically opposed to tai chi chuan, which is structured: Choreographed. Precise. Repetitive. Lovely, but very different from our Western mentality. Movement meditation resembles jazz more.

In 1985, long before the Tiananmen Square riots, I participated in a cultural exsimple change in China. I observed children drawing fish in Beijing's children's palaces. They would consistently catch a carp. The carp appeared identical to me. Young children demonstrated various martial arts with exceptional discipline. Orderly. Repetitious. Subtle.

We have much to learn from Eastern culture, and they have much to learn from us. We are undergoing a time of redefinition.

Redefining limitations. Personal. Political. Each individual has so much to teach the other.

However, it must just begin with the body. And for us in the West, the body must just take the lead – free form.

Don't overreally do it. Less is more. The power will arrive. Be committed to the procedure. Every day, put your mind out of the way and allow your body to embody your spirit.

I enjoy playing music during my movement meditation. Nothing loud or rhythmic, because then the music will instruct my body, and I want my body to communicate with me. No, I prefer tranquil, legato music, whether classical, new age, Indian, or indigenous.

Some of the stretches my body has required have astonished me; my feet and toes have been the most instructive, my spine has been full of surprises, and my abdominal muscles have spoken volumes.

While practicing the mundane, body and spirit rise above the mundane.

When a man of his word married, as his second wife, the most proud and haughty woman ever seen, she already had two daughters from a previous marriage who were, without a doubt, identical to her. In addition, he had a young daughter from a previous marriage who inherited her mother's unrivalled goodness and pleasant disposition.

As soon as the wedding services concluded, the reception began. However, through marriage, the mother began to reveal her true nature. She was unable to tolerate the admirable qualities of this lovely young woman, all the more so because they made her own daughters appear more repulsive. She employed her in the most menial tasks of the household: she scrubbed the dishes, tables, etc., and cleaned the lady's chamber and those of the misses, her daughters; she slept in a dank attic on a pathetic straw bed, while her sisters slept in opulent rooms, with floors generally trimmed, on beds of the most modern design, and where they had mirrors so large they could see themselves from head to toe.

The unfortunate young lady took it all in stride and tried not to tell her father, who may have run through her, as his wife completely administered him. When she had completed her duties, she would go into the chimney stack corner and sit among the soot and ashes, which earned her the nickname Cinderwench. However, the youngest, who was not as impolite and rude as the oldest, referred to her as Cinderella. Cinderella, despite her shabby attire, was significantly more attractive than her sisters. However, they were such always attired in opulence.

It transpired that the Lord's child hosted a ball and invited all well-dressed individuals. Our young ladies were also well-received, as they cut an exceptionally fine figure among the competition. They were extremely ecstatic to receive this greeting and were extraordinarily busy selecting outfits, slips, and headwear that suited them. This was yet another obstacle for Cinderella, as she was the one who ironed her sisters' clothing and plaited their unruly hair; they spent the entire day discussing how they should be dressed.

"As for me," said the eldest, "I'll be wearing my red velvet suit with French management."

"Also, I," said the youngest, "will have my standard slip; however, to easy make up for that, I will wear my gold-bloomed cloak and my precious stone stomacher, neither of which are the most common."

They contacted the best tyre lady they could simply find to fix their hoods and replace their double pinners, and they received their red brushes and repairs from Mademoiselle de la Poche.

Cinderella was also called upon by them to advise them on a variety of matters, as she had excellent ideas and constantly encouraged them to really do the right thing. Furthermore, she offered to dress their heads, which they were eager for her to do. While she was doing this, they asked her, "Cinderella, are you not excited to attend the ball?"

"Oh my goodness!" she exclaimed, "you easy make fun of me; it's not like I'm going there."

"Thou art is morally deserving of it," they replied; "it would amuse people to see a Cinderwitch at a ball."

Anyone other than Cinderella would have dressed improperly. However, she was excellent in general and dressed them perfectly. They had gone approximately two days without food due to their excitement. They broke more than twelve bands while attempting to be tightly bound so that they could have a fine, slender figure, and they were glued to their mirror. Finally, the happy day arrived; they went to court, and Cinderella followed them with her eyes for as long as she could before she lost just focus and began to cry.

When her guardian saw her crying, he asked her what was wrong.

"I want to - I want to - "; she was unable to finish her sentence due to her tears and sobbing.

This backup parent of hers, who was a pixie, told her, "Thou art wise enough to attend the ball; is it not so?"

Cinderella responded with an incredible murmur, "Yes."

"Well then," said her guardian, "behave as a proper young lady, and I will arrange for your departure." Then, she brought her into her room and instructed her, "Run to the garden and bring me a pumpkin."

Cinderella hurriedly gathered the best pumpkin she could simply find and carried it to her guardian, unable to imagine how this pumpkin would enable her to attend the ball. Her backup parent removed everything from the pumpkin, leaving only the skin. Once this was accomplished, she struck the pumpkin with her wand, and it was instantly transformed into a gold-plated mentor.

She then went to investigate her mouse trap, where she discovered six mice, all of which were alive. She asked Cinderella to lift up the hidden entrance while giving each mouse a little tap with her wand as it exited; the mouse was instantly transformed into a fine pony, resulting in an exceptionally fine arrangement of six mice-colored dappled-dark ponies. Cinderella, who has been mistaken for a coachman, says, "I will just take a quick trip to see if there will never be a rodent in the rodent trap - we may easy make him a coachman."

"Thy craftsmanship is justifiable," her backup parent responded; "continue to observe."

Cinderella brought the trap to her, which contained three enormous rodents. The Pixie chose one of the three with the most facial hair, and after contacting him with her wand, he was transformed into a fat, jovial mentor with the smartest bristles eyes ever observed. From that point forward, she shared with her: "Return to the nursery, and behind the watering can you will simply find six reptiles; bring them to me."

She had just completed doing so when her guardian transformed them into six footmen who scurried up quickly behind the mentor, dressed in gold and silver, and stuck as closely together as if they had never done anything else in their entire lives. The Pixie then said to Cinderella, "Indeed, you see here a carriage fit for the ball; would you say you're not pleased?"

"Oh my goodness!" she exclaimed; "however, should I go there in these horrifying garments?"

Her adoptive parent barely touched her with her wand, and in the same instant, her garments were transformed into gold and silver fabric adorned with jewels. She then presented her with the most beautiful glass shoes in the entire world. Being thusly attired, she ascended into her mentor;

however, her backup parent ordered her not to remain until after 12 PM, telling her that if she stayed one second longer, the mentor would transform back into a pumpkin, her ponies would turn into mice, her coachman would turn into a rodent, her footmen would turn into reptiles, and her attire would return to its previous state.

Chapter 6: Guidelines, And Frequently Asked Questions Regarding The Practice Of Vipassana

Taking a Seat for Meditation

Where is the best location for meditation? Buddha suggested that the best place for meditation is a forest, under a tree, or another extremely quiet location.

How should I sit when I meditate? Buddha advised meditators to cross their legs and sit quietly and peacefully.

What if I have back problems or other sitting difficulties?

If sitting with crossed legs is painful or difficult, other seated positions can be utilised. A chair is acceptable for those with back issues when meditating. Sit with your back straight, at a 90-degree angle to the ground, but not rigidly.

Why is sitting upright so crucial?

The reason for sitting upright is straightforward. Sitting with an arched or crooked back will cause pain and discomfort over time. In addition, the physical effort required to remain upright without additional support energises your meditation practise.

Why is sitting position so crucial?
To achieve mental peace while meditating, we must ensure that our bodies are at ease. Therefore, it is essential to choose a position that will allow us to remain comfortable throughout practise.

Inhalation for Meditation

After sitting, what is the next step?
Close your eyes. Then, just focus your attention on your abdomen, or belly.

Normalize your breathing by not forcing it, neither by slowing it down nor by speeding it up. Simply a normal breath.

What should I be mindful of when I breathe?

As you breathe in and your abdomen rises, and as you breathe out and it falls, you will really become such aware of the sensations throughout your entire body.

Why is breathing essential?

Vipassana uses the breath as a focal point, besides the obvious. Your breath is a vital reference point; when your mind wanders, you can use it to bring it back. More on concentration in the following section.

Increasing Concentration for Meditation

How can I sharpen my just focus and aim? You can improve your just focus and concentration by ensuring that your mind is attentive to each phase of your breathing. Ensure that you are immediately such aware of all sensations associated with breathing. Maintain a consistent level of just focus throughout the entire just beginning, middle, and conclusion.

Although we describe breathing, specifically the rise and fall of the abdomen, as having a just beginning, middle, and end, this is only to demonstrate that your awareness should be continuous and comprehensive. These processes are not intended to be divided into three segments. Rather, you should attempt to be conscious of each of these movements from just beginning to end as a single, continuous process.

Why is it essential for Vipassana meditation to have both effort and a clear focus?

It is necessary to exert effort and pay close attention in just order for your mind to directly and powerfully perceive the sensations you experience.

How should one respond when their mind just begins to wander?
Watch your thoughts. You must be such aware of your own thoughts.

How really do you clear your consciousness of thinking?
Note the thought in silence and verbally label it "thinking," and then return your just focus to your breath and the rising and falling of your abdomen.

5. Is it possible to maintain perfect concentration on the breath at all times?

No, nobody can realistically maintain perfect concentration on their breath indefinitely. Other objects will eventually emerge and really become predominant in the mind. Thus, meditation encompasses all of our experiences, including sights, sounds, smells, tastes, bodily sensations, and mental objects such as the imagination and emotions. When any of these arise, you should direct your attention to it and use a soft verbal label.

Chapter 7: Tips For Establishing A Regular Meditation Practice

Developing a regular meditation practise can be difficult, especially for those who are new to the practise. However, with some commitment and effort, it is possible to incorporate meditation into your daily routine. Here are some suggestions for establishing a regular meditation practise:

Each day, set aside a specific time for meditation. Setting aside a specific time each day for meditation, such as first thing in the morning or just before bed, can be beneficial. This will help you incorporate it into your routine.

Simply find a quiet, comfortable space. In just order to fully relax and concentrate during meditation, it is essential to simply find a peaceful, undisturbed location. This could be a meditation room or a quiet corner of your home.

➢ Just begin with a few minutes daily. If you're new to meditation, it can be beneficial to just begin by meditating for only a few minutes per day and gradually increase the length of your sessions as you gain comfort with the practise.

Employ a guided meditation. There are numerous resources that provide guided meditations if you are uncertain of where to just begin. These can be useful for teaching you the fundamentals of meditation and providing a structure to adhere to.

➢ Maintain constancy. The key to making meditation a regular practise is to continue it even on hectic or stressful days. Even if you only have a few minutes to meditate, try to meditate daily at the same time and don't skip sessions.

➢ Be tolerant of yourself. It is essential to just keep in mind that meditation is a skill that requires time and practise to acquire.

Really do not really become disheartened if you struggle to concentrate or if your mind wanders during your sessions. With time and practise, your meditation skills will improve.

Meditation has numerous benefits, including the reduction of stress and anxiety, improvement of just focus and concentration, and promotion of overall physical health. By designating a specific time each day for meditation and remaining consistent with your practise, you can incorporate meditation into your daily routine.

overcoming common difficulties and obstructions

It can be difficult to incorporate meditation into your daily life, especially if you are new to the practise. When attempting to easy make meditation a regular part of their routine, individuals encounter a number of obstacles and difficulties. Here are some suggestions for overcoming these obstacles and incorporating daily meditation into your life:

The ability to simply find the time. Finding the time to meditate is one of the greatest obstacles people face when attempting to incorporate meditation into their daily lives. Setting aside a specific time each day for meditation, such as first thing in the morning or just before bed, can be beneficial. This will help you incorporate it into your routine.

Focusing one's attention. Keeping one's concentration is a typical obstacle for those who meditate. It is normal for the mind to wander during meditation, but with practise, you can learn to rejust focus on your breath or a mantra. Using guided meditation can also be useful for maintaining focus.

Handling interruptions. It is essential to simply find a peaceful, undisturbed location for your meditation practise.

However, even in the most conducive environments, distractions can occur. When this occurs, attempt to recognise the distraction and let it go without becoming engrossed in it.

➢ Continuing to really do so. The key to making meditation a regular practise is to remain consistent, even on hectic or stressful days. Even if you only have a few minutes available, it is important to be consistent and not skip sessions.

Having patience with oneself. It is essential to just keep in mind that meditation is a skill that requires time and practise to acquire. Really do not really become disheartened if you struggle to concentrate or if your mind wanders during your sessions. With time and practise, your meditation skills will improve.

Incorporating meditation into your daily life and reaping the many benefits of this practise can be facilitated by overcoming these common challenges and obstacles. You can easy make meditation a regular part of your daily routine by setting aside dedicated time, remaining focused, dealing with distractions, persevering, and having patience with yourself.

Chapter 8: The Connection Between Your Mind And Emotions

How to help your child manage his or her emotions

As your child experiences various emotions, you can assist him or her in recognising and naming them. If your child is feeling down, he or she can locate the sad-looking frog on the card. Here are some questions that can help you demonstrate your curiosity and initiate a discussion about your emotions:

Can you pinpoint the precise location where you just feel it? Which type of response really do you prefer? Are you prepared to sit with such an emotion and allow it to wash over you, as you might with a beloved pet or longtime friend?

When we allow ourselves to experience the present emotion, we just begin to recognise its characteristics. Once again, the emotions of sadness have shifted. This is something I can concentrate on. This is very helpful. Additionally, children can benefit from learning that they can "survive" or endure difficult emotions. It is equally important that your children recognise and value your anxiety, irritation, restlessness, sadness, and exhaustion. After a long day, you might still have enough energy to play one more game. "All right, this is the last one!" Occasionally, you are simply not in the mood. You are exhausted and desire nothing more than to sit and rest. Likewise, that is also acceptable.

Chapter 9: Developing Psychic Capabilities — The Third Eye

Your third eye chakra is located directly on the forehead, just above and between the eyebrows. It is known as the Ajna. It is responsible for intuition and foresight, and it functions when you allow yourself to be receptive and constantly engage your imagination. According to Yoga metaphysics, it is the centre of your "I" persona, which is distinct from the rest of the world. It is purple in colour and reminiscent of moonlight.

Om is the symbol for this chakra. In Hinduism, Krishna, the God of Wisdom, oversees this chakra. When you chant Om, you stimulate the Ajna, which helps you focus, grounds you, and makes you such aware of the Divinity in every aspect of life. This is not surprising, as Om is the seed from which all creation sprouts.

In addition, the symbol contains an inverted triangle and a lotus flower, both of which represent wisdom. The triangle represents the development of wisdom within you. It symbolises the expansion of your understanding, which brings you closer to spiritual enlightenment. In Hinduism, the lotus flower is associated with Brahma, the God of Creation. It represents the splendour of life, fertility, success in all your endeavours, and eternity. Ajna is a chakra composed of shades of indigo, deep blue, and violet. When these hues are combined, they convey mystique, intelligence, faith, loyalty, and kingship.

This chakra is associated with the pineal gland, which has the shape of a small pine cone and is located in the brain. It is responsible for producing melatonin in the body, which is why, assuming you listen to your body, you can sleep and wake up at the appropriate times.

When your Ajna is out of balance, you are unable to see clearly and have difficulty thinking clearly. You reject out of hand anything spiritual or mystical. It is difficult to have faith and trust that things will work out when you cannot see the big picture and really become so fixated on minute details.

Your Ajna receives no support from the other chakras when it is overactive, causing you to really become lost in a world of illusion and pure fantasy. As a result of your out-of-balanced chakra, you have difficulty defining your life goals because you lack vision. Therefore, you must such always ensure that this chakra is balanced. The longer you allow it to continue, the more disconnected you really become from reality and the more likely you are to end up in a straitjacket. As much as the physical world is an illusion, you are here and a part of it, so it would be prudent to respect it as an independent reality. Spirituality and physicality should coexist in your life, and you should not prioritise one over the other.

When this chakra is out of balance, you experience intense fear when you see visions, which depletes you on all levels (physically, emotionally, and mentally). In addition, you suffer from insomnia, nausea, seizures, sinus issues, vision problems, and excruciating headaches. You will learn later in this chapter how to open your third eye and maintain its equilibrium.

This gland is the Pineal Gland

This gland is the link between the physical and spiritual realms. It can assist you in igniting your supernatural abilities and employing them for your own purposes. It is the source of the ethereal energy necessary to fully develop your psychic abilities. Additionally, the pineal gland interacts with the hypothalamus, an additional gland that regulates thirst, hunger, sexual desire, and your biological clock. It is the third eye, and it functions in tandem with the pituitary gland.

Your Ajna is the source of your inspiration, creativity, unique wisdom and insight, connection with extraterrestrial beings, and sense of vision. This chakra allows you to access your intuition and exercise your psychic abilities, including clairvoyance, clairaudience, and more. It allows you to see auras and other forms of energy all around you.

When you awaken this chakra, your inner world of perception will be rich. You will see visions, the nature of which will depend on how you perceive them. Sometimes the vision is hazy, and sometimes it is crystal clear.

The pineal gland receives more blood than any other organ in the body, and it is also surrounded by cerebrospinal fluid. Melatonin is present in high concentrations. This melatonin is an anti-stress and anti-aging antioxidant. It is also the reason you sleep well at night. It regulates your disposition, immune system, and circadian rhythms. It is a photosensitive gland, which means that light and darkness affect its production of melatonin. Light inhibits its production of melatonin, whereas darkness promotes its production.

When the gland releases melatonin into your system, it circulates around your brain and then travels through your blood vessels to all parts of your body. If you really do not consume enough melatonin, you will experience mood swings, depression, and other seasonal disorders. Melatonin is also responsible for breaking down chemicals in the brain such as pinoline and DMT, which regulate physical and emotional processes, respectively.

Chapter 10: Typical Impediments To Meditation:

A discussion of the common obstacles people face when just beginning a meditation practise and how to overcome them.

For some individuals, just beginning a meditation practise can be difficult, and they may face a number of common obstacles. Here are some frequent obstacles and advice for overcoming them:

If you have difficulty sitting still for extended periods, try incorporating movement into your meditation practise, such as walking meditation or yoga.

It is normal for the mind to wander during meditation; if you simply find it difficult to concentrate, try focusing on a mantra or an object, such as a candle flame or a crystal.

If you experience boredom or restlessness during meditation, try incorporating some variety into your practise by experimenting with different types of meditation or by listening to guided meditations.

If you experience physical discomfort during meditation, such as back pain or neck tension, try adjusting your posture or supporting your body with a cushion or bolster.

If you have a hectic schedule, it can be difficult to simply find the time to meditate. Easy make meditation a priority and incorporate it into your daily schedule. Even brief meditation sessions can be beneficial.

If your mind is constantly racing and you simply find it difficult to calm it, try not to worry. Simply observe your thoughts and allow them to pass you by like clouds in the sky, without becoming entangled in them.

By understanding common obstacles and employing the aforementioned strategies, you can overcome obstacles and develop a consistent, effective meditation practise. Remember that meditation is a journey, and be patient and kind with yourself as you learn and develop.

Chapter 11: Just Keep The Outcomes In Mind

Everything that threatens the ego is liberating to the heart, according to the British dharma teacher Jahn Amaro. It's a nod to the notion that meditation loosens us up and helps us let go of our habitual ways of thinking and behaving, making it easier for us to express our genuine emotions. Allowing yourself to experience terror is counterintuitive, but it can be beneficial. As previously stated, Trungpa Rinpoche characterised emotion as "energy mixed with concepts." You have sufficient self-assurance to drop the subject or end the conversation. Just keep in mind that while overwhelming emotions may distract you from your meditation practise, they will not cause you to delve deeper into your own emotional experience. In actuality, the opposite of what you might expect to occur when you just focus on breathing into a strong emotion is true. That is exactly what occurs. As soon as we experience an intense emotion, our minds and bodies go into action, which distracts us from the experience.

I have spent the preceding chapters attempting to persuade you that experiencing genuine emotion is a prerequisite for awakening and living a more authentic life. This practise, known as "postmeditation," is performed after meditation and should be maintained throughout the day. You may be the type of individual who finds sitting in meditation to be nothing but a relaxing experience. This is a normal part of the training process that affects everyone, particularly in the just beginning. During duty rotations at retreats, when people are forced to work with people they dislike or easy make phone calls they would rather avoid, resentment reaches a boiling point. Consider that your emotions may seize you by the collar and misdirect you in the minutes following your meditation.

Emotional arousal impairs our ability to concentrate. Attention training is the process whereby we learn to pay attention to the present moment without judging or overanalyzing it. We are participating in training designed to heighten our awareness. We are training for a gentle, receptive reception of all sensory information (thoughts, sights, sounds). Complete acceptance of whatever is present in the room at the time. However, the emergence of strong emotions has a way of distracting us from the task at hand. When meditating, one's mind may wander in a million different directions if they are distracted by intense emotions that prevent them from concentrating on their breathing.

When this occurs, we frequently resort to combative coping mechanisms, such as assigning blame to others or dwelling on our own shortcomings through "they," "me," or "if only" stories. Looking for ways to cause harm, pointing fingers, and exacting retribution are all possible outcomes. We must just begin future planning immediately. On the other hand, we may attempt to calm ourselves using techniques we have learned to employ when experiencing intense emotions. We attempt to shield ourselves from unpleasant experiences by establishing emotional distance. By watching television, eating mindlessly, and obsessively pursuing other forms of pleasure, we zone out from life. As a result, we may spend a great deal of time worrying about how to avoid facing or experiencing it. We may really become distracted by recalling past experiences or imagining potential future events. We may also convince ourselves that we're great, that we will easy make things right, that we're in the right, etc., in just order to just feel better. When we employ any of these techniques, we really become further removed from an actual and immediate experience of the event.

When experiencing intense emotions, we may also retreat inward. We employ a variety of strategies to shape events and ensure a positive outcome. When there are numerous tangential sensations vying for our attention, it is easy for the primary feeling to get lost in the shuffle. The initial fear we experience is the most intense, followed by subsequent emotions such as grief, paranoia, jealousy, anger, and dread. Trying to simply find a way out of this situation is becoming increasingly difficult. Illness is just one of the forms that evasion strategies can take. To my misfortune, I've been feeling quite ill. People who frequently use illness as a tactic may come to view it as a strategy, despite the fact that it is typically not done on purpose. You succumb to an intense emotion that overpowers you. Utilize your illness to your advantage, despite feeling guilty about it. Consider the critical thoughts that arise when anger escalates. Uncertainty surrounds the conclusion of the stories you tell yourself. Really do you have a tendency to overthink things? How gentle are you with yourself when this emotion resurfaces? When working one-on-one with students, I frequently hear them being critical of themselves when they just begin to experience strong emotions during practise. I frequently hear the phrases "I can not really do this," "I never really do it correctly," and "This is too difficult." You may be saying to yourself, "This strategy is ridiculous," or to the world, "This is a waste of my time." We frequently engage in a variety of self-destructive thought patterns.

Therefore, I typically advise my students to stop trying to easy make sense of everything and instead concentrate on the present, rather than relying on any of the competing explanations. You may regain your composure by focusing on your breathing as you attempt to store the memory in your brain. The phrase "hold the experience" does not imply that the listener should attempt to bottle the event. To let down one's guard and reveal one's true self to another person requires courage. The courageous decision to preserve the memory instils in us and all other living things an innate sense of generosity.

When you allow yourself to experience all of your emotions, you will discover a whole new world of understanding, love, and compassion.

Chapter 12: Limit Your Time Observe Your Body

Now, let's examine some of the activities you can incorporate into your daily routine to achieve higher mental levels (i.e., greater brain power and clarity!).

FIRST PART: IMPROVING YOUR MIND

An efficient daily routine enables you to maintain laser-like just focus from the moment you wake up in the morning until you close your eyes and drift off to sleep at night. Here are several ways to obtain it:

Start the day with a positive mantra. Positive thinking, according to the Mayo Clinic, reduces stress and improves health.

"Today will be the greatest day ever!"

I just begin each day by uttering (out loud) these simple words as soon as I get out of bed. Yes, I even tell myself this on mornings after too short of a night's sleep or when I awaken feeling like the weight of the world is on my shoulders. Why?

These nine phrases put me in the proper mindset for the upcoming day.

It is not the events that easy make a day pleasant or unpleasant, but rather your attitude toward them. Jim Rohn once said, "You either run the day or the day runs you."

I want to immediately put my mind in GOOD condition...

because, if left unchecked, it will try to tell me FALSE information...

But with a positive attitude, I can overcome it.

Benjamin Franklin used to ask himself daily:

Choose a statement or question that rings true for you. It may be as simple as smiling and saying "Thank you" aloud, and being grateful for another day.

Be proactive: Really do not first check your email!
Really do you check your email and social media accounts as soon as you wake up in

the morning? If so, you just begin your day in a reactive rather than proactive mode.

According to Jocelyn K. Glei in Manage Your Day-to-Day, the problem with this strategy is that it requires spending the majority of the day on other people's priorities.

If you receive an email requesting work-related documents, for instance, you may just feel compelled to provide them immediately...

despite the fact that you had intended to market your side business. Or, if you open

Facebook and see one of your friends in a crisis, you may lose just focus on your own problems or concerns.

You will be in a much better state to assist others and accomplish more throughout the day if you just begin each day by focusing on YOU.

Psyche yourself up: Visualize your success
Some of the greatest athletes in the world use visualisation to mentally prepare themselves to excel in their sport. In a 2011 interview with USA Today, Aaron Rodgers, basically considered by many to

be the best quarterback in the NFL, discussed the power of visualisation.

Jack Canfield, co-author of the Chicken Soup for the Soul series, recommends 10 minutes of daily visualisation to "harness the power of your subconscious mind."

Simply close your eyes and visualise yourself excelling and being the greatest version of yourself. Imagine yourself in situations where you excel and visualise the best possible outcome. Include as much detail as possible in your images, employing all of your senses to easy make your "training" more effective.

For those who have trouble closing their eyes and "seeing anything," I recommend using a pen and paper to write out how you want your day to progress. Be as descriptive as possible...while taking care to remain positive.

All of this is intended to transmit commands from your conscious mind to your subconscious mind. Your subconscious mind wants to believe what you tell it (whether positive or negative), and it will really do whatever it takes to easy make those directives a reality.

Even if it is just a page, read a book.

There are many scientific benefits to reading books. Reading may increase your IQ, your brainpower (for up to five days, according to research conducted at Emory University), and even your ability to empathise with others. Reading has also been found to reduce the risk of Alzheimer's disease by more than twofold, while simultaneously reducing stress.

The bestselling author of Simplify, Joshua Becker, has made it his mission to read one book per week because reading makes him a better leader, broadens his worldview and expands his knowledge, and strengthens his self-discipline.

I don't know about you, but I simply find it challenging to read an entire book. Who has countless hours per day or week to simply sit and read?

Therefore, I commit to reading only one chapter of a book of my choosing each day. I'm currently reading several different novels, so I simply select the one that appeals to me the most that day and sit down to read a chapter. If I desire to read more, I will.

By breaking the enormous task (reading an entire book!) into manageable chunks (one chapter), I can read approximately 50 books per year.

Employ a partner or a mentor to hold you accountable

I have a mentor whom I contact daily. Even if I only send him a message, this small task holds me accountable. In addition, it compels me to just keep myself (and my thoughts) moving in the right direction.

If you really do not currently have a mentor, you should consider how to acquire one. Or simply find someone you can trust to be your accountability partner, someone who will hold you to your word. The Hip-Hop Preacher, Eric Thomas believes accountability partners are essential for success, and his accountability partners have impacted his life:

ET suggests compiling a list of three individuals in whom you have confidence and respect. Explain to each of these individuals precisely what it is that you wish to accomplish. After the conversation, determine which of these individuals would serve as the best accountability partner for the specific milestone you are attempting to achieve.

Ensure that they will also benefit from the transaction. Author Ryan Holiday wrote, "Bring something to the table."

"Anything. Quid pro quo. Even if it's just energy. Even if it's only a thank you You cannot continually request without providing anything in return. The greater the payoff you can offer, the longer they will protect you. Determine what you can offer and provide it. Here's a freebie: Then they won't waste time searching for relevant articles and books.

www.ingramcontent.com/pod-product-compliance
Lightning Source LLC
Chambersburg PA
CBHW050300120526
44590CB00016B/2426